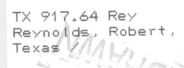

TEXAS

BY ROBERT REYNOLDS

TEXAS

International Standard Book Number 0-912856-10-6
Library of Congress Catalog Card Number 73-75619
Copyright © 1973 by Publisher • Charles H. Belding
2000 N.W. Wilson • Portland, Oregon 97209 • 503/224-7777
Designer • Robert Reynolds
Copy Editor • Thomas Worcester
Printer • Graphic Arts Center
Binding • Lincoln & Allen
Printed in the United States of America
Second Printing

Storm-swept prairie in Terry County.

Cottonwood tree in Crosby County.

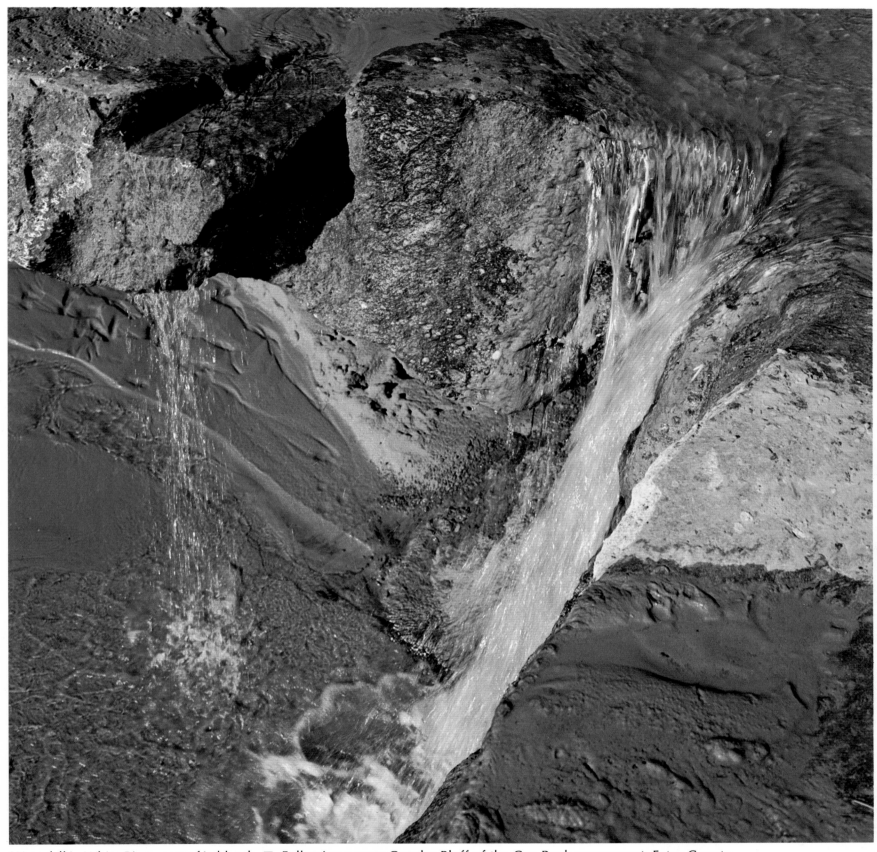

Waterfall in White River, east of Lubbock. □ Following pages: Concho Bluff of the Cap Rock escarpment, Ector County.

Highway on Great Prairie, near Lamesa.

Early maple buds in McKittrick Canyon, Guadalupe National Park.

Field yucca in Hudspeth County.

El Capitan, southern tip of Guadalupe Mountains.

High desert from Hueco Tanks State Park.

Ancient Indian grain grinding holes in Winkler County.

Cornudas Mountains, from Dry Salt Lake, Hudspeth County.

Leathery hands of an old vaquero.

Stained glass window in San Elizario Mission, El Paso County.

Ysleta Mission, El Paso.

Limestone wash in Black Gap, Brewster County.

Flowering Engelmann prickly pear, Big Bend National Park.

Bighorn sheep, tarantula, and road runner in Black Gap, Brewster County.

Rocky Pass in Chisos Mountains, Big Bend National Park. □ Following pages: Winter-tinted bushes on sand dunes, Winkler County.

Gilberto Luna House, Big Bend National Park.

Strawberry cactus in Big Bend National Park.

An old ranch wagon in Culberson County.

University of Texas' McDonald Observatory, Davis Mountains.

Catching up a horse at daybreak, Delaware Mountains.

Horse taking a cool dip in a water hole in Culberson County.

Riders line out for a day's work in the Delaware Mountains.

Bluebonnets on prairie near Laredo.

Church tower in Los Ebanos, on the lower Rio Grande.

Mesquite, a dominate foliage in south and west Texas.

Hand-drawn ferry on lower Rio Grande at Los Ebanos.

Huisache bush in Spring near Falcon Lake.

Portuguese man-of-war on beach at Boca Chica.

Shrimp boat on the ways at Port Isabel. ☐ Following pages: Wind-bent live oaks on shore near Rockport.

Driftwood on beach of Padre Island.

White-tail deer in Aransas.

American alligator, a nearly extinct species, in Aransas National Wildlife Refuge.

Morning sun over the broad coastal plain north of Corpus Christi.

Barren live oak at Aransas National Wildlife Refuge.

Fleecy clouds above hills north of San Antonio.

Remains of old homestead and stone wall in hill country west of Austin.

A young oak coming on in the spring, Burnet County.

Waterfall on Curry Creek, Kendall County.

Unique architectural decoration in the old German community of Fredericksburg.

House of hand-hewn timbers and native rocks built in 1856, Fredericksburg.

Wall decoration, Mission San Jose, San Antonio.

Mission San Jose, a Texas State and national historic site.

Monument to the men of the Alamo, San Antonio.

Shoreline on Lake Buchanan, Llano County.

Hill country west of Austin, Lake Lyndon B. Johnson in background.

Recreation boat on Lake Travis.

The Enchanted Rock of Llano County, 500 feet high, 640 acres of Texas pink granite.

Exotic wildlife ranch near Boerne.

Early morning light on Lake Raven, Huntsville State Park.

Fall leaves of a post oak in Brazos Valley.

A bronze of the father of Texas, Stephen Fuller Austin, at San Felipe.

Anson Jones Home, Washington on the Brazos.

The Big Thicket, Polk County.

A farm in Sam Houston National Forest.

Country lane, Upshur County.

Campground in Davy Crockett National Forest. □ Following pages: Morning fog on lake at Tyler State Park.

Sparkling sun on Lake o' the Pines, Marion County.

Fog-shrouded trees on the banks of the Sabine River, Wood County.

Scarlet leaves of sumac in Palo Pinto County.

Country road in dense forest of East Texas near Marshall.

Lions in drive-through zoo. ☐ Jet take-off over Dallas. ☐ Dallas skyline. ☐ Purple sage.

Dallas from the air.

Interstate bridge over the Red River north of Gainesville.

Scuba diver exploring the shoreline of Lake Texoma.

Prickly pear cactus and longhorn steer, Fort Griffin State Park.

Beginning of fall on a hillside near Mineral Wells.

Floor hands pulling sucker rods on an oil well service unit, Scurry County.

Cotton on the high prairie near Memphis in Hall County.

Schackelford County courthouse in Albany.

Longhorn at old Fort Griffin. □ Following pages: Cowboys return to ranch, north of Abilene.

Chuck wagon on prairie near Guthrie.

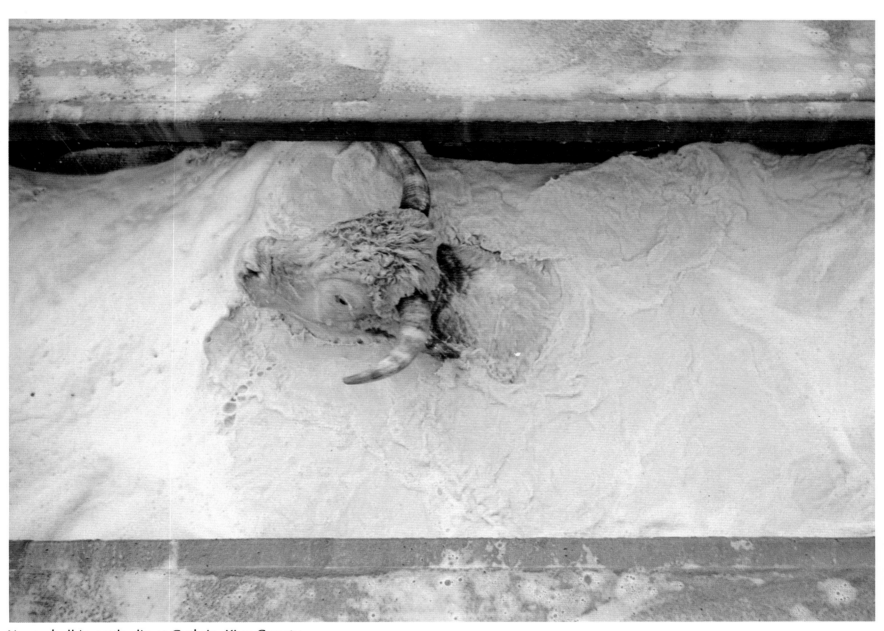

Young bull in cattle dip at Guthrie, King County.

Double Mountain Fork of the Brazos River, Garza County.

Herd of bulls, King County.

Prickly pear in bloom, Throckmorton County.

The prairie town of Matador.

Combine and wheat in Texas Panhandle, Hartley County.

Lightning and great thunderhead over the plains near Levelland.

Sunset through cottonwood trees, Palo Duro State Park.

Escarpment of the Great Plains in Palo Duro State Park.

Miniature Oak or shinnery in Ward County.

The prairie near Andrews after a summer storm. ☐ Following pages: Sandhill crane in Muleshoe National Wildlife Refuge.

Cultivated fields north of Lubbock.

Farmlands near Hereford.

A fence post on the plains, home for a grasshopper.

Barbed wire fence in Deaf Smith County in the Texas Panhandle.

Cotton fields near Littlefield.

Grain elevator on Route 66 near Vega.

Oil rig south of Andrews.

Highway at night near Notrees, west of Odessa.

Sundown in Monahans Sandhills State Park.

A blooming cholla in Davis Mountains.

McKittrick Canyon, Guadalupe Mountains National Park.

Century plant, Guadalupe Mountains.

Remains of the old Butterfield Stage stop at Pine Springs, Culberson County.

Long spine prickly pear, Big Bend National Park.

Sierra Diablo Mountains, Hudspeth County.

Rio Grande at Langtry.

Wall at San Elizario Museum, El Paso County.

Painted Desert in Big Bend National Park.

Creosote bush, a dominant plant in the Trans-Pecos.

Roadbed of the old Overland Stage Route in the Delaware Mountains.

Storm clouds roll in over the Guadalupe Mountains.

Cowboy pulling off a bridle after a day's work in the Delaware Mountains.

Highway in Culberson County north of Van Horn.

Breakfast fire on a Culberson County ranch.

A ranch remuda, Trans-Pecos.

Suburbs of El Paso below the Franklin Mountains.

Lassoing a mount from a rope corral on a Delaware Mountains ranch.

Guadalupe Mountain National Park.

Antelope, sheep, and goats share pasture land. ☐ Rugged mountains on the River Road east of Presidio.

Polished granite at the rockpile in the Davis Mountains, in background Sawtooth Mountains.

Chinati Mountains in Presidio County.

Torrey yucca in bloom, Big Bend National Park.

Chisos Mountains of Big Bend National Park.

The Davis Mountains, Jeff Davis County.

Coralloid formations in the Sonora Caverns.

Fort Worth skyline from a gallery of the Amon Carter Museum.

A country store at Justiceburg in Garza County.

Sweetgum leaves and pond in the Mission Tejas State Park.

Moss on a post oak tree, Titus County.

Moss on cypress trees in Caddo Lake.

Old pine tree in the Davy Crockett National Forest.

Sundown near Tyler in Smith County.

Tranquil East Texas setting on the Alabama and Coushatta Indian Reservation.

Loblolly pine tree, Sabine National Forest.

Fall trailings of pine, sweetgum and post oak.

Camping among the pines in Sabine National Forest.

In Galveston; playing in the surf, and century-old architectural designs.

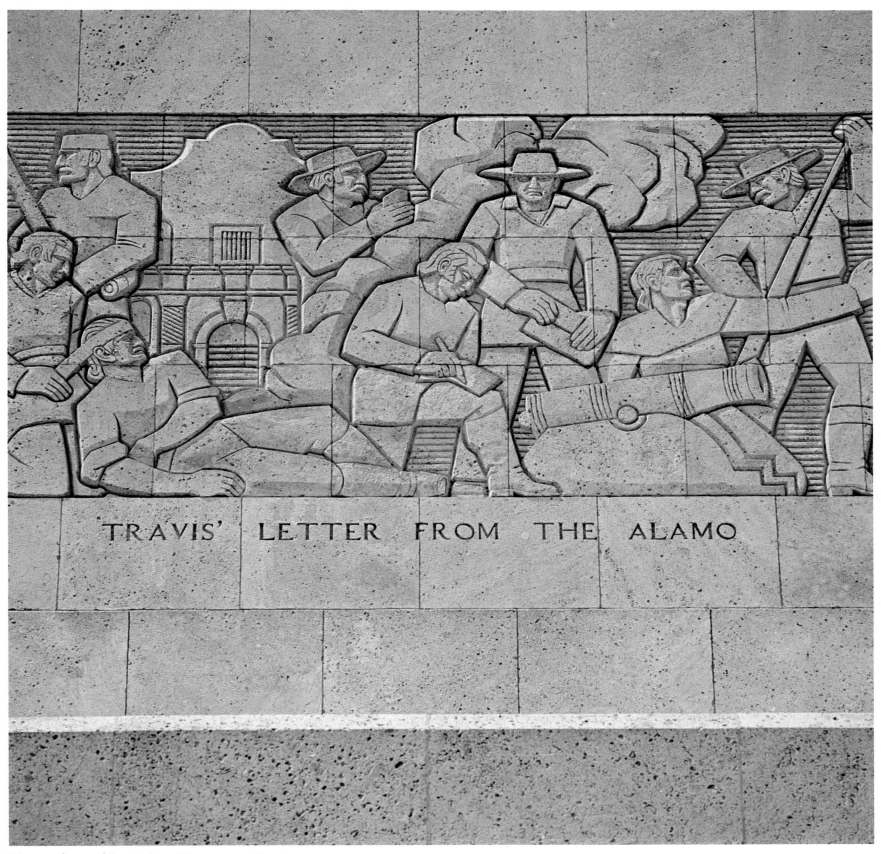

Frieze at base of San Jacinto Monument, Houston.

Ashton Villa in Galveston, constructed 1858.

Great Blue Heron greets the morning sun on Galveston Island.

Houston skyline from Sam Houston Park.

Palms in the lower Rio Grande Valley near McAllen.

Leopards at rest in a Brownsville Zoo.

Fields of Indian Blanket at Baffin Bay in Kleberg County.

Aransas, winter feeding ground of hundreds of migratory birds. □ St. Joseph Island on the Gulf.

Roseate spoonbills on the Intercoastal waterway, Aransas.

American alligator in Aransas Wildlife Refuge.

Common egret in a coastal marsh at Rockport.

Live oak in garden of L.B.J. Library, Austin.

Sam E. Johnson farmhouse on L.B.J. Ranch, birthplace of President Johnson.

Stone column on a wing of Mission San Jose, San Antonio.

Bell tower of Mission San Juan, San Antonio, Bexar County.

Edge Falls on Curry Creek north of San Antonio, Kendall County.

Feedlot near Johnson City, Blanco county.

Monument to the Texas Cowboy on the Capitol Grounds, Austin.

Bluebonnet sprinkled with raindrops.

TEXAS: An Afterword

The central plains of North America intrude more than two hundred miles into Texas before the land drops to a lower prairie. Woodlands of the American south, thick in pine and sweetgum, make a green belt for one hundred and fifty miles west of the Sabine River in Texas. Trailings of the Rocky Mountains protrude in great rock piles above the high desert floor of southwest Texas. Fresh, swift rivers bubble from limestone hills around the Edwards Plateau, to struggle across the coastal plains to the Gulf of Mexico.

A white-tailed deer dips its graceful body under a fence, then bounds into a protective thicket of cedar. A herd of pronghorn antelope browse knee-deep in grammer grass high in the Delaware Mountains. A vee shaped flight of sandhill cranes returns to the warm and protected waters of Aransas.

The Dry Salt Lake west of the Pecos, a flowering yucca in Black Gap, a ponderosa pine in McKittrick Canyon, a waterfall in the Guadalupe River, moss on a cypress tree in Caddo Lake, the skyline of Houston or Dallas or Fort Worth, a sidewalk cafe in San Antonio, the 19th century German architecture in Fredericksburg; these are some of the things of Texas.

The Texan, known afar for his independence, seems to gather his strength from his environment. The well-groomed cosmopolitan women in a shop in Austin or Dallas reflect the knowing ways of a highly civilized culture, yet a cowboy pushing a cow out of the rough brushy country, in West Texas works much as his grandfather did, relying on moxie and a good horse.

Historically, the vastness of this land and the climate which permeates it has developed men for whom the boundaries were limited only by the strength of their mounts or the hardships they were willing to endure. Prior to the coming of the white man, the Comanche and Kiowa Indians traveled over great expanses from the Panhandle to Old Mexico, gathering wealth in horses, and in bison.

The Spanish missionaries were self-sufficient, too, for they established their Christian outposts in hostile territory, many leagues beyond the economic assistance of Mexico City. That same independence can be seen in the Anglo farmers who settled the Brazos Valley, for they, too, could not depend on outside help. Survival was in working the land.

So the Texan today reflects the spirit of his various ancestors, as if his independence comes from knowing the land and listening to the winds of change that contour the modern life.

These, then, are some of the things of Texas.

MARY AUSTIN HOLLEY
1836
University of Texas Archives

Texas, until within the last few years, has been, literally, a terra incognita. That such a region existed, has, indeed, been known; but in respect to its geography and natural resources, clouds and darkness have rested upon it. This is the more remarkable, lying as it does, contiguous to two enlightened nations, the United States, on the one side, and Mexico, on the other; being, moreover, very easy of access, both by land and sea. While Britons, impelled by a daring spirit of enterprise, have penetrated to the ice-bound region of Melville's Island, and our own New Englanders have encountered all the hardships and hazards of the western desert, the Rocky Mountains and hostile Indians, to find a home at the mouth of the Columbia river, this most inviting region, lying just at their doors, has been altogether overlooked. Quite unexpectedly, as it were, a report has reached the public ear, that the country lying west of the Sabine river, is a tract of surpassing beauty, exceeding even our best western lands in productiveness, with a climate perfectly salubrious, and of a temperature, at all seasons of the year, most delightful . . .

While listening, for the first time, to the favourable reports of Texas, it must be confessed, a suspicion is very apt to arise in the mind, that so much imputed excellence if it really existed, could not have been so long concealed from the view of the world; and we are prone to ask, how has it happened, that a territory, possessing such uncommon advantage of climate and soil, has not been explored and appropriated before? To this very natural enquiry, a satisfactory answer is at hand.

Two causes seemed to have operated to prevent the earlier settlement of the province of Texas, and to retard the development of its resources. In the first place, the jealous policy of the old Spanish government, uniformly discouraged all attempts to penetrate into the country. It was the policy of the government, that completely locked up Texas, and all the Spanish American possessions and excluded even visitors and travellers. It was a favorite saying of the Spanish Captain General of the Internal Provinces, Don Nemisio Salcedo, that he would stop the birds from flying over the boundary line between Texas and the United States, if it were in his power. This rigid policy prevented any one from attempting to explore the country by land, for perpetual imprisonment was the inevitable result of detection and capture.

In the second place, the Carancahua Indians, who inhabited the coast, were represented to be of a character, uncommonly ferocious. They were, popularly, believed to be cannibals, and many tales of most frightful import, were told of them; such as, if true, it must be acknowledged, were sufficiently appalling to check the enterprise, and damp ardor of the most eager adventurer. These representations of the character of the Carancahuas, though, in a measure true, were greatly exaggerated; and it is believed by many, that they were either fabricated or at least countenanced, by the Spanish authorities, to prevent intercourse with the Province, which it was not easy to guard by a military force. Thus, the whole of this country remained for ages unknown to the world, and instead of being converted into an adobe of industrious and happy freemen, at is might have been, it was doomed by the selfishness of men, to continue a howling wilderness. No maps, charts or geographical notices, were ever allowed by the Spaniards to be taken of it. The map compiled by Gen. Austin, and published by Tanner, was the first geographical information of the country, that was published. . . .

It is uncertain how long this extensive and valuable country would have remained unknown and unsettled, had not the bold enterprise and perseverance of the Austins torn away the veil that hid it from view of the world, and redeemed it from the wilderness, by the settlement of a flourishing colony of North Americans, on the Brazos and Colorado Rivers. With the settlement of this colony, a new era has dawned upon Texas. The natural riches of this beautiful province have begun to be unfolded, and its charms displayed, to the eyes of admiring adventurers. A new island, as it were, has been discovered, in these latter days, at our very doors, apparently fresh from the sands of its Maker, and adapted, beyond most lands, both to delight the senses, and enrich the pockets, of those who are disposed to accept of its bounties.

Without any assistance from the government, or fostering care of any sort, but simply under a permission to enter, many thousands of industrious farmers and mechanics, with their families, have located themselves here. Their numbers are rapidly increasing, and there cannot be a doubt, that, in a few years, Texas will become one of the most thriving, if not the most populous, of the Mexican States.

LETTER OF GENERAL SAM HOUSTON, TO GENERAL SANTA ANNA
University of Texas Archives

Executive Department,
City of Houston, March 21, 1842

Most Excellent Sir:

Your communications to Mr. Bee and General Hamilton, dated at the Palace of the Government of Mexico, have been recently presented to my notice. At the first convenient leisure I have not failed to appropriate my attention to the subjects embraced within the scope of your remarks . . .

Whatever opinions you may have entertained in relation to the difficulties existing between Mexico and Texas cannot materially vary the facts and principles involved, nor will they materially influence the decision of mankind upon the justice of our cause. . . .

The people of Texas were invited to migrate to this country for the purpose of enjoying equal rights and constitutional liberty. They were promised the shield of the constitution of 1824, adopted by Mexico. Confiding in this pledge, they removed to the country to encounter all the privations of a wilderness under the alluring promises of free institutions. Citizens of the United States had engaged in the revolution of Mexico in 1812. They fought gallantly in the achievement of Mexican independence, and many of them survive, and to this day occupy the soil which their privations and valor assisted in achieving. On their removal here they brought with them no aspirations or projects but such as were loyal to the constitution of Mexico. They repelled the Indian savages; they encountered every discomfort; they subdued the wilderness, and converted into cultivated fields the idle waste of this now prolific territory. . . .

You can well imagine the transition of feeling which ensued on your accession to power. Your subversion of the constitution of 1824, your establishment of centralism, your conquest of Zacatecas, characterized by every act of violence, cruelty, and rapine, inflicted upon

us the profoundest astonishment. We realized all the uncertainty of men awakening to reality from the unconsciousness of delirium. In succession came your order for the Texans to surrender their private arms. The mask was thrown aside, and the monster of despotism displayed in all the habiliments of loathsome detestation. Then was presented to Texans the alternative of tamely crouching to the tyrant's lash, or exalting themselves to the attributes of freemen. They chose the latter. To chastise them for their presumption induced your advance upon Texas, with your boasted veteran army, mustering a force nearly equal to the whole population of this country at that time. You besieged and took the Alamo; but under what circumstances? Not those surely, which should characterize a general of the nineteenth century. You assailed 150 men, destitute of every supply requisite for the defense of that place. Its brave defenders, worn by vigilance and duty beyond the power of human nature to sustain, were at length overwhelmed by a force of 9,000 men, and the place taken. I ask you sir, what scenes followed? Were they such as should characterize an able general, a magnanimous warrior, and the President of a great nation numbering eight millions of souls? No. Manliness and generosity would sicken at the recital of the scenes incident to your success, and humanity itself would blush to class you among the chivalric spirits of the age of vandalism. This you have been pleased to class in the "succession of your victories:" and I presume you would next include the massacre at Goliad. . . .

So far as I was concerned in preserving your life and subsequent liberation, I was only influenced by considerations of mercy, humanity, and the establishment of a national character. . . .

But you declare that you will not relax your exertions until you have subjugated Texas; that you "have weighed its possible value," and that you are perfectly aware of the magnitude of the task which you have undertaken; that you "will not permit a Colossus within the limits of Mexico;" that our title is that of "theft and usurpation," and that "the honor of the Mexican nation" demands of you "the reclamation of Texas;" that "if it were an unproductive desert, useless, sterile, yielding nothing desirable, and abounding only in thorns to wound the feet of the traveler, you would not permit it to exist as an independent government. . . ."

Sir, from your lenity and power Texans expect nothing—from your humanity less; and when you invade Texas you will not find "thorns to wound the foot of the traveler," but you will find opposed to Mexican breasts arms wielded by freemen of unerring certainty, and directly by a purpose not to be eluded. Texans war not for gewgaws and titles; they battle not to sustain dictators or despots; they do not march to the field unwillingly, nor are they dragged to the army in chains, with the mock-title of volunteers. For a while they lay by the implements of husbandry, and seize their rifles; they rally in defense of their rights; and, when victory has been achieved, they return to the cultivation of the soil. They have laws to protect their rights. Their property is their own. They do not bow to the will of despots; but they bow to the majesty of the constitution and laws. They are freemen indeed. . . .

You tauntingly invite Texas to cover herself anew with the Mexican flag. You certainly intend this as mockery. You denied us the enjoyment of the laws under which we came to the country. Her flag was never raised in our behalf, nor has it been seen in Texas unless when displayed in an attempt at our subjugation. We know your lenity— we know your mercy—we are ready again to test your power. You have threatened to plant your banner on the banks of the Sabine. Is this done to intimidate us? Is it done to alarm us? Or do you deem it the most successful mode of conquest? If the latter, it may do to amuse the people surrounding you. If to alarm us, it will amuse those conversant with the history of your last campaign. If to have harassed our citizens—you have incarcerated our traders, after your commissioners had been kindly received, and your citizens allowed the privileges of commerce in Texas without molestation—you continue aggression—you will not accord us peace. We will have it. You threaten to conquer Texas—we will war with Mexico. . . . If experience of the past will authorize speculations of the future, the attitude of Mexico is more "problematical" than that of Texas.

In the war which will be conducted by Texas against Mexico, our incentive will not be a love of conquest; it will be to disarm tyranny of its power. We will make no war upon Mexicans against the authorities of the country, and against your principles. We will exalt the condition of the people to representative freedom; they shall choose their own rulers; they shall possess their property in peace, and it shall not be taken from them to support an armed soldiery, for the purpose of oppression.

With these principles, we will march across the Rio Grande; and believe me, sir, ere the banner of Mexico shall triumphantly float on the banks of the Sabine, the Texan standard of the single star, borne by the Anglo-Saxon race, shall display its bright folds in liberty's triumph of the Isthumus of Darien.

With the most appropriate consideration, I have the honor to present you my salutation.

SAM HOUSTON.

To his Excellency ANTONI LOPEZ DE SANTA ANNA, President of the Republic of Mexico.

---

from
ON A WESTERN RANCHE
by J. BAUMANN
Fortnightly Review, April 1887

The Cowboy has at the present day become a personage; nay, more, he is rapidly becoming a mythical one. Distance is doing for him what lapse of time did for the heroes of antiquity. His admirers are investing him with all manner of romantic qualities; they descant upon his manifold virtues and his pardonable weaknesses as if he were a demi-god, and I have no doubt that before long there will be ample material for any philosophic inquirer who may wish to enlighten the world as to the cause and meaning of the cowboy myth. Meanwhile the true character of the cowboy has become obscured, his genuine qualities are lost in fantastic tales of impossible daring and skill, of dare-devil equitation and unexampled endurance. Every member of his class is pictured as a kind of Buffalo Bill, as a longhaired ruffian who, decked out in gaudy colours and tawdry ornaments, booted like a cavalier, and chivalrous as a paladin, his belt stuck full of knives and pistols, makes the world to resound with bluster and braggadocio. From this character the cowboy of fact is entirely distinct. It is true he is brave and independent; he is reckless of his own life, and pays small heed to the lives of others; but he is not of those who seek the bubble reputation of meaningless folly and overbearing swagger. He is in the main a loyal, long-enduring, hard-working fellow, grit to the backbone, and tough as whipcord; performing his arduous and often dangerous duties, and living his comfortless life without a word of complaint about the many privations he has to undergo. I have myself lived with him on his lonesome prairies, I have shared his fatigues and his pleasures, and taken part in the many moving incidents of his life, and I have no hesitation in warning any restless, roving spirits who may be attracted by picturesque descriptions of a cowboy's life that, unless they are prepared to toil during the long summer months, both by day and by night, for small pay and on scant fare, to be in the saddle from early dawn until sunset both Sundays and weekdays to abstain from comfort and civilization for the greater part of every year, and so to wear themselves out with exposure and manifold fatigues as to be reckoned old and past their work whilst still young in years, they had better remain at home and leave cowboy life alone.

ADVENTURES WITH A TEXAS NATURALIST
by ROY BEDICHEK
from University of Texas Press,
copyright 1947, revised edition 1966

Toward the end of each August I have an attack of Davis Mountain Fever. Nothing will do it any good except a visit there for a week or two weeks, or just as long as I feel that I can afford to stay.

The summer tourist with Davis Mountains as a destination is forced into an enjoyment of immediate and quite surprising contrasts, since every approach, except by air, is so guarded that he is fairly exhausted by the time he gets there. It is a long pilgrimage from any one of the more populous centers in Texas. I have tried every route. Coming in by the Del Rio-Devil's River way, you get to see the awful gash cut in the stone by the lower reaches of the Pecos; and you have hills chalky and for the most part barren and "not worth a damn," a cowboy told, "except to hold the world together." These white hills are hot and monotonous, and the road weaves around and over them, and then along and across flat-bottomed arroyos channeled out by freshets on their way to the Rio Grande. Finally, somewhere between Sanderson and Marathon ,the whitish soil turns red, gray hills turn green, and you have reached the tip of a cool finger of the Rockies. Now for fifty miles or so the hills become higher and greener, and the air is sweeter and cooler. The introduction by this route is more gradual, hence the contrast is slightly dulled.

From the west—that is, from El Paso—the road courses the Rio Grande for nearly a hundred miles, keeping to the edge of the desiccated foothills while yet in sight of river verdure which serves to underscore the desert and make the traveler more fully conscious of it. Finally this highway cuts through the breaks to Van Horn, and then follows another hundred miles, mostly desert, rather featureless. Of course, one might trickle down from New Mexico through the Guadalupe Mountains due south, but, once in the pleasant Guadalupes, the temptation is to let well enough alone and camp there for the duration. There remains Highway 290, due west from Austin, which runs across the Edwards Plateau to Sheffield, bad enough in August, and then for a hundred and fifty miles the country is typical Trans-Pecos.

I prefer the road of the most violent contrasts: the Bankhead Highway, U.S. 80 to Pecos, thence south to Balmorrhea and on up Limpia Canyon into the mountains.

I can assure the August tourist that, if he takes this route, he will arrive well-baked, so weary from looking over plains alternating with greasewood flats glazed with alkali, and peering into the mirage shimmering down long stretches of overheated pavement, that his eyes will welcome anything to lean upon. When, finally, the mountains are recognized—first mistaken for a bank of cloud along the southwestern horizon—the spell begins to take hold.

This past summer I left Dallas and the Trinity Bottom one bright August morning and, driving conservatively, reached Sweetwater for lunch. I faced the sun that afternoon for another two hundred miles and still had enough energy left to make camp on my own power among the sand dunes near Monahans. I left the highway, following an old road which led me to the site of some wildcatter's dream and disillusionment, a cleared-out space among the dunes littered with oil-drilling debris.

I found myself in the midst of a miniature forest of oak and mesquite. Each dune is crowned by an oak tree, ten to twenty-four inches tall, loaded with acorns. Interspersed among the oaks and towering above them is scrub mesquite, heavy with clusters of long, yellowish beans hanging nearly to the ground.

I venture the statement, without research, that in no other forested section, the Amazon Valley not excepted, is there to be found a higher proportion of fruit to wood than in this Lilliputian jungle in the northern portion of Ward County. Vegetatively considered, it is as much a natural curiosity as the Painted Desert or the wonder-areas of Yellowstone. This hummocky expanse of stunted growths, or an ample sample of it, should be reserved and protected as a state or national park.

Dr. B. C. Tharp informs me that the little oak (Quercus havardii) is confined to the sandy South Plains of Texas and of eastern New Mexico. Rarely reaching a height of thirty inches, its slender stems arise from a thick rootstock buried four to eight inches below the surface. It bears a fat acorn nearly an inch long and more than half an inch thick. Thus the old proverb, "Great oaks from little acorns grow," is reversed in this topsy-turvy land where only miniature oaks from giant acorns grow.

The transformation of the genus Quercus as one passes from East to West Texas is a demonstration in ecology that he who runs may read. Other genera doubtless present as conspicuous adaptations to the practiced eye of the botanist, but not to the casual observer, for oaks are spectacular, even dramatic.

Certainly the live oak (Quercus virginiana), noblest tree of Texas soil, appears in this trek from east to west in a greater variety of disguises than any other oak. Rows of live oaks adorn long stretches of Texas gulf shore, following its sinuosities, rooted in immense sand dunes, where they are beaten in the face, so to speak, by the salt spray whipped up by the violent gulf winds. This has the effect of stunting their gulfward exposure but permitting their landward growth to continue unimpeded. Thus after years of facing the salt spray they present as perfect a picture of streamlining as can be found anywhere in the vegetable world. In profile and particularly in twilight they look like regiments of maenads fronting the sea, with long tresses blown backward toward the land, sculptured by the prevailing winds.

A little way inland, the same species grows to enormous proportions. A specimen near Rockport is said to be the largest tree of any kind in the state. Still farther inland, reduced in size, they assume regular proportions, achieve an immense spread supporting graceful festoons of Spanish moss, and constitute the most prized lawn tree of a wide belt skirting the coastal prairie southwestward for a hundred miles, roughly from Houston to Victoria.

Still further reduced in height but not in spread, and therefore squattier in appearance, the live oak ranges across the southern half of the Edwards Plateau and remains an outstanding feature of the landscape. Here it emphasizes the habit of extending its limbs horizontally until the weight of the foliage tends to depress the tips to the ground fifty or more feet from the trunk. Wherefore Walt Whitman called it a "loving lounger in my winding path"; and indeed it does seem to lounge rather than stand. Locally, however, throughout the Plateau, this aged giant is often reduced to the status of a mere bush or shrub.

Again, a Texas white oak (q. breviloba) takes curious shapes as it leaves the river bottoms and struggles up tributary creeks, finally mounting slopes of shallow soil and insufficient moisture where the species is ill-suited to the competition it encounters. Once atop the limestone ridges, it becomes definitely dwarfed. But in shady creek bottoms where cedar elms, green ash, pecans, vines, and other shade

producers thrive, this white oak begins a hopeless search for a place in the sun. It twists and turns this way and that in pursuit of sunshine, frustrated and indecisive as one growth after another, beats it to a promising position. It is headed off here and there, back and forth, until it becomes so deformed as to be scarcely recognizable as a tree at all. Its bole sometimes makes a right-angle turn and skews off in one direction or another, around and about, writhing like a wounded serpent, and offering a very good representation of arboreal agony after the manner of the Laocoön group.

Also, wherever the sturdy post oak and blackjack leave the congenial sandy soils and invade the limestone hills, they become scrub oak, not more than twenty feet tall.

And finally, as a last gasp of genus Quercus in its due westward extension in non-mountainous country, we come upon the most spectacular adaptation of all, a species weed-sized, perhaps the least oak in the world — Harvard's oak, sharing with the mesquite the apparently sterile sands and, in spite of terrific winds, holding these sands in comparatively stable dunes.

Here I found hogs of normal size browsing on acorns in the tip-tops of this pigmy white oak. I followed for a short distance an immense sow with litter of eleven pigs, her nose barely skimming the sand, apparently searching for something. It turned out that she was water-witching and to good purpose, for presently she began rooting. Soon her long, vigorous snout unearthed a spring of crystal-clear water—a result quite as miraculous to me at the moment as the sight the thirsty wanderers in an ancient desert beheld when their leader "lifted up hand and with his rod smote the rock twice." This water the sow and her well-mannered progeny sipped, after the manner of swine that are permitted a free range. Hoggishness, gulping, and filth are forced upon this naturally dainty beast by close confinement and competitive feeding in the most degrading animal slums. Instead of the folk simile for filth, "dirty as a hog," we should say "dirty as the hog's keeper."

Having satisfied the family thirst in this leisurely manner, sipping and savoring the cool spring water, she lay down in it, cooling her belly and, turning first this way and then that, extended the grateful moisture as far up her immense sides as possible. Thus refreshed, and now slightly suspicious of my continued interest, she wandered on with a gurgle of soothing grunts to keep her brood closely huddled about her; for there is the strange carnivorous creature, man, and also the sly coyote abroad, either of whom has been known to snap up and make off with a straying and too adventurous suckling. So she disappeared among the dunes while loose and flowing sand crept in and covered up the spring to filter and keep it uncontaminated for the next patron. It was told that hogs get killing fat here, feeding on acorns and watering from their rooted-out springs in the sand. The popularity in West Texas of the so-called "tall story" is often a mystery to me. There are so many incredible facts there lying around on the surface that the manufacture of the tall story is a futile exercise of the imagination. It's a matter not only of transporting coals to Newcastle, but of delivering a cheap grade of lignite.

Early anthropologists were mystified, it is said, by litters of Indian camps — flint slivers, chips, cores, scrapers, arrowheads and other artifacts — scattered about in this sandy desert. "No water, no kitchen middens" is a maxim of anthropological explorations in Texas, and this apparently ancient water supply was discovered a foot or two beneath a surface of dry and blowing sands.

I turned from this sagacious sow to note a cactus wren relining its nest. Before I became acquainted with this species, I had always thought of the wren as quite a midget among birds. I had grown up with the Texas Bewick wren, small and dapper, gray like a mockingbird and marked like him, except for the mocker's wing-spots. I knew the Carolina wren, of course, a little larger than the Bewick, of rich coloring and of bolder song. Familiar, also, was the canyon wren as well as the rock wren, fuller of curiosity than is any other member of the tribe which is noted the world over for prying into affairs which are none of its business.

I had had fleeting glimpses of the marsh wrens; and from late fall to early spring, we have throughout central and eastern Texas the winter wren, tiniest of them all, which stripped of its feathers, is no bigger than your thumb.

But here in the Monahans mesquite, among other marvels, is a huge wren, almost as big as a robin; and he scolds from afar in an unwrenlike voice that is often mistaken for the bark of an angry rodent. The little winter wren could be hovered under this bird's wing; indeed, the winter wren from tip to tip is but a trifle longer than the tail of this giant species.

There were three other nests in the same mesquite, clustered near the one my bird was relining, each with its side entrance, and each one bigger than a man's head. I thought I had the only case on record of nesting colony of wrens until I was advised by Mrs. Merriam Bailey that other observers had formed the same erroneous conclusion. There is only one real nest in the shrub: the others are dummies to fool lizards, mice, and suchlike stupid, homeless ones, sleepy and seeking a lodging for the night. The male wren, it is said, sometimes sleeps in a dummy nest while his mate is brooding.

Cattle fare as well as hogs in this part of Ward County. Cowmen have told me that there are times when not a fat range steer is to be found anywhere between Fort Worth and El Paso except in the Monahans sands. I am told also that the cattle grown on this soft terrain, which yields to the slightest pressure, cannot be driven afoot on hard ground for the reason that their hoofs grow to such lengths that the moment these members are put on a resistant surface, they break and bleed. In pretrucking days this was a serious marketing inconvenience.

Horses are not so happy here, or at least were not during my last visit. There had been barely two inches of rainfall in seven months and the range was short. Horses were lean and had turned to gorging themselves on mesquite beans, occasionally dying of a colic. A veterinarian told me that his chief income during droughty summers is derived from dosing horses for overdoses of beans.

Of course, now the Monahans country is thought of only as an oil field; but the old-timers still think of it in terms of fat hogs and tender-footed cattle.

Across Ward County westward from the sand dunes, north of the highway and still east of the Pecos River, high on a desert mesa, are marks, designs, and figures called petroglyphs, pecked into the surface of smooth, flat-topped rocks. The aborigines, who chose these rocks upon which to indite their letters to posterity, seem to have run more to geometry than to anatomy—that is to say, geometrical designs predominate over human and animal representations. However, rude caricatures of both man and beast occur, as well as lines suggestive of tools or weapons or obviously symbolic figures—all fascinating to look upon.

What a dismal place, this mesa, overlooking a far-stretching valley, scantily clad in ragged, semiarid growth! Winding through it runs a sudden little river, deceptively clear, tempting the thirsty, but bitter as gall. Here, where one would least expect it, is this indisputable evidence of an urge in the savage mind to communicate, to leave a record—faint echo from a distant past, hint of an imagination striving to make its vision manifest.

These and similar writings scattered pretty generally over parts of western Texas always bring before my mind the figure of a man—it's always a man, never a woman—sitting cross-legged on a stone, leaning forward with back bent like a bow, tangled hair dangling about his cheeks, eyes burning with an inward light and intent upon his strokes as, stone hammer firmly grasped, he pecks away with a terrific determination to set down the recollection of some dream, or remembered forms, or images seen through a glass darkly—or maybe simply a trail-marker.

In spite of all the learned speculations concerning what these and similar writings may mean, much is left to guess and surmise. Little wonder! Give Leonardo da Vinci or Praxiteles or Walt Disney a stone hammer without a handle, a flat rock on a wind-swept mesa for a canvas, and a steady diet of meat, cactus apples, and mesquite beans, and I doubt if any one of them could make himself more intelligible.

It may be that this primitive artist and thinker lacked only the writer's alphabet, brush and canvas, marble and chisel, or the cinema mechanisms and organization. Maybe modern progress has been only in tools, materials, and technique and not in mentality itself. Anthropologists, generally, believe there is no indication that the modern mind in and of itself is in any way superior to that of human beings who lived forty thousand years ago. They attribute present wonders to the flowering of a long accumulation of facilities, to the coral-like deposition of agelong successions of myriads of minds, cultural inheritances, and so on.

But this is not the place or the season for indulging the dreams that relics or records of a prehistoric past inspire. The rocks this August afternoon are too hot to sit down upon. The light falls with such intensity as to rob the landscape of its charm. A certain amount of physical comfort is necessary, anyway, to fruitful speculation. Spring is not the time, either: season of winds driving sharp dust across these exposed mesas with such abrasive violence as eventually to erase the record, some say, and wipe the ancient slate clean.

But even so, all will not be lost after the winds of centuries have done their worst. Under the direction of the late Professor J. E. Pearce, Mr. A. T. Jackson and his many helpers have collected and published two volumes comprising more than nine hundred pages wherein with pen and camera thousands of Texas pictographs are preserved. This Ward County location is officially designated as Site No. 50.

Volume II of this work contains a map showing the distribution of counties of Indian picture-writings, a glance at which suggests that prehistoric West Texas was much more literate than East Texas of the same period. But sectional pride should not be stimulated by this circumstance, since the writing materials of the west are more durable and the climate more favorable than those of the east for the preservation of such records. Nature supplied the prehistoric literates of East Texas with fragile materials—inkberry juice and bleached pine logs in some instances—as well as with a moldy climate. Few evidences of picture-writings occur east of the Colorado River, and hardly a scratch east of the Trinity.

No, the philosopher should stop by Site No. 50 later, in the fall of the year, say, when the land is cooled down in a tempered sunlight and has become quiet as only the desert can become—calm without stir or motion and with a meditative haze resting upon the purplish horizon. Then, with sufficient leisure and toward sunset when the sheer vastness of the landscape seems designed as a mete and measure for eternity itself—just then, with physical conditions right, he might with feeling or intuition, not with thought, get a glimpse of the significance of these curious messages, as of rappings coming to the faithful through a spiritualistic medium. Maybe it is in tiny rivulets such as this that the great river of human communication has its source; maybe we have found here a birth spring of artistic creation, hidden from the eye deep in the cavernous past, and inaudible except to the sympathetic ear alert in the desert stillness to catch its natal murmur.

Beasts have left us records from a million years ago: tracks, rubbings, wallows; aimless, idle pawings in the primeval mud; but how many worlds away in purport are these scratches and scrawls left by the human hand, for in them is perceived the mind of man responding to creative impulse. In such rude markings we get intimations of a will to create, of the mind's budding ability and determination to impress itself upon materials, communicate its thoughts, visions, dreams, to demonstrate that, as the poet declares, the mind is "a thousand times more beautiful than the earth on which it dwells," and that truly and in fact, it is.

WHAT IS A TEXAN?
by R. Henderson Shuffler
from an address before the
International
Convention of
Torch Clubs
San Antonio, 1973

When I was growing up in Northwest Texas, more than half a century ago, our real national holiday was April 21st, San Jacinto Day. We paid our respects to the Fourth of July by firing an anvil and listening to an oration or two, but, with so many old Confederate veterans still among us, too much bearing down on the glories of the Union was a touchy thing.

San Jacinto Day was ours, and ours alone. The old boys in grey who had won all the battles and still lost the Civil War (to hear them tell it) and the Indian fighters who had lost a lot of their battles and still actually won their war, could celebrate the victory of San Jacinto with unmixed ardor. They had heard the whole glorious story from the lips of their fathers and grandfathers, who had been there "the day we whupped ole Santy Anny," and they would pass it on, with proper embellishments, to any who would stand long enough to hear it.

Every San Jacinto Day people from miles around would gather in to a little clearing for an orgy of visiting, milling about, over-eating, and sheer wonderment of the sight of so many people, horses, mules, and dogs all together. There were band and fiddle contests, wrestling matches, tugs-of-war and foot-races. Maybe even an impromptu baseball game, if anyone had thought to bring a ball and bat. (Those horny-handed old-timers disdained the use of gloves and mitts.)

The highlight of the celebration was "The Speaking," an interminable assortment of old-time, full-throated oratory emanating from a bunting-draped platform in the very middle of the grounds.

Those old-time orators were something: leather-lunged, silver tongued, and unbelievably tireless. They had never heard of a microphone—and why did a man who called in cows from the far pasture every night need an electronic booster to be heard by a few hundred people, all standing right in front of him?

On one of these sun-drenched San Jacinto days a bull-voiced orator had been spellbinding for an hour and a half. He had fought the Battle of San Jacinto, blow-by-blow, sung a few bars of "Will You Come to the Bower," and signed the Declaration of Independence right there in front of us. He had made the welkin ring with his praises of old Sam Houston and polished the Lone Star until it shone like the noonday sun.

At a peak of emotion and eloquence, he sang out:

"Texiss, my friends, is a land where every man is just as good as every other man!"

At this point an old-timer on the front row was completely carried away. He jumped up, threw his hat in the air and yelled back:

"You danged tootin', Mister! . . . and a damned sight better!"

That is Texas for you. Someone has described it as, not just a State of the Union, but a practically ecstatic state of mind. The late George Perry labeled it "Texas, A World in Itself." It has been called an empire, a geographic giant—and a lot of things much less flattering.

Texas is a land of amazing diversity in terrain and climate and astounding wealth of natural resources. But it is not the land which makes Texas so distinctively different. Our plains region is merely an extension of the Great Plains of the midwest, our coastal area is a part and parcel of the great Gulf crescent from Florida to Mexico. Our piney woods are simply the western edge of the great Southern forests. The mountains of far West Texas are a part of the Rockies and the Chisos of the Big Bend belong to the great mountain chains of Mexico.

Nor does the difference lie solely in our people, who have come here from all parts of the world and are of the same stock and traditions as those of their homelands.

The one unique Texan attribute is the myth to which we cling, a myth of our own creation, which the world at large has accepted and now feeds back to us, often to our dismay. It all started in fun, as old Texans snowed newcomers with lusty tales of such "practicing characters" as Strap Buckner and Brit Bailey, Big Foot Wallace and Three-Legged Willie, with indestructible Peg-Leg Ward thrown in for good measure. These people all lived in early Texas, and at least a part of what was told of them was true. But embroidering the truth with imaginative fiction is what made the stories good. "Lore," after all is simply the past-perfected of "liar."

Aylett C. "Strap" Buckner, the red-haired giant of a frontiersman who settled on a creek near the Colorado in what is now Fayette County around 1819, must have been a hardy soul, to survive in the wilderness for so long. He may even, as they tell it, have felled a giant black ox with one blow of his fist—but it is extremely doubtful that he ever actually whipped the Devil in a fair fist fight on the riverbank at midnight.

Brit Bailey, who came into the Coastal country well before Austin's Old 300, was also a mighty eccentric fellow, quick to quarrel and ready for a fight. It is believed to be true that he was buried standing up, with a jug of liquor between his feet and a rifle in his hand, because he didn't want anyone coming around and saying "There lies Old Brit Bailey." He had never looked up from a prone position to any man while he was alive, and didn't aim to, dead. But it is doubtful that Old Brit still comes back at night, to roam the prairie, looking for a refill for his jug. (That's probably only swamp gas the storytellers have seen.)

And Peg-Leg Ward did lose a leg at the siege of Bexar. (It was said to have been buried with Ben Milam.) Then he went back to New Orleans, strapped on a peg leg, recruited a company of volunteers, and led them valiantly at San Jacinto. On the second anniversary of that battle, he and Sam Houston and several others were celebrating the victory with a bibulous party at the town of Houston and decided to fire a cannon. Somehow they shot off Ward's right arm, leaving him completely lopsided. After that he served with glory as the land commissioner of Texas. But it isn't true, as they sometimes tell it, that Peg-Leg Ward whipped Frank Lubbock with his crutch, standing on one leg and using his only remaining arm, while Lubbock held a six-shooter on him.

These are all good Texas yarns, each with its grain of truth, but each enhanced by every successive teller until it became folk myth. The trouble with myths is that they so often outlive the truth, and finally are mistaken by succeeding generations for historic fact.

Over the years, many of these folk myths have degenerated into what is know as "Texas Brags!"—corny, ill-conceived boasts, as boresome as they are windy. They have earned Texans a reputation in many parts of the world with which we could well dispense.

In any modern book, magazine article, stage play, movie or television show, a character identified as a Texan is immediately recognized as an object of laughter—or fear—or both. He is either a new-rich fool who happened to fall into a barrel of oil and come up smelling like a millionaire, an autocratic cattle baron who has wrung his riches from the souls of the little people who are his serfs, or a clever, conniving wheeler-dealer who amassed millions by fiscal crapshooting with crooked dice. The fictionalized Texan is always violent, vain, loud and laughably unlettered. And this is the role in which we have been cast, with only minor variations, since the beginnings of our history.

The early Texian has always been pictured to the world as a bumpkin in buckskin, a rough-cut character of the half-horse, half-alligator school, who came romping across the Sabine in 1821, kicking the Mexicans and Indians out, to take over the wilderness and build an empire. He is traditionally shown as an Anglo-American from the South—a hard-drinking, loud-swearing and long-praying lout, two jumps ahead of the sheriff because of a recent killing, or a very old debt.

If this were the truth—or even a half-truth—Texas would be a wilderness still.

David Crockett, the boisterous, wry frontiersman in his coonskin cap and ragged buckskins, who feared neither man nor beast, so long as he had his trusty rifle by his side and his lethal hunting knife (or equally lethal liquor jug) in hand, was the prototype of the mythical early Texian.

That Davy Crockett was the sheerest fiction. The character he portrayed was created by a second-rate New York playwright and promoted by eastern politicians. He first appeared in a play on the New York stage in 1830, as a flamboyant frontiersman named Col. Nimrod Wildfire, principal of the farce called "Lion of the West."

Whig politicians, frightened by the amazing popularity of home-spun Andrew Jackson, desperately wanted to create a folk hero to outshine the President. They cast Crockett in the real-life role of Nimrod Wildfire and he played it to the hilt. He made the phony backwoodsy campaign speeches written by the party hacks and developed the rustic eccentricities required by the character he had assumed. He even sanctioned the awkwardly-contrived books and Almanacs which were published in his name, though written by low-grade eastern ghosts. The money these antics brought, he needed; the fame he thoroughly enjoyed.

But David Crockett was no more like Nimrod Wildfire than was the average early Texian. An examination of the extemporaneous speeches he made during his three terms in Congress and the letters he wrote which are still in existence, proves Crockett to have been a quite literate man. He used none of the curious backwoods expressions with which the hack writers had adorned his fictionalized reminiscences and campaign speeches. He was grammatical, sensible, and civilized.

The only time he posed for his portrait in what he described as his "real hunting garb," Davy did not wear a coonskin cap. He held in his hand a large felt hat of the type worn by most of the frontiersmen of his time. And on the eve of his departure from Tennessee, Crockett wrote a little-known poem, expressing his sorrow at leaving the land he had helped to tame. It was grammatical, literate, and flawless in meter.

So much for the fictional ancestor of the mythical Texan. It is true that Texas had some pretty rough-cut characters on the frontier in the 1820's and '30's. It is also true that many of them were playing roles, just as Crockett did. Big Foot Wallace, who is always portrayed as one of the roughest-hewn of the early Indian fighters, was really the scion of a very distinguished old Tidewater Virginia family. His name was William Alexander Anderson Wallace. He clowned and ripped and roared on the frontier, in greasy buckskins and shaggy hair and beard. But when he went home for a visit, Wallace always stopped off in New Orleans, dressed up in the latest fashion, had himself tonsored in the newest style, and went back to Virginia as a gentleman.

Erastus (Deaf) Smith, the taciturn scout and hunter, was a New Yorker of more than common education. The lovely quatraine he wrote on the death of Ben Milam was a classic in early Texas letters. The truth is that the Texas frontier society of the 1820's and 1830's was as exciting and cosmopolitan as the world has ever seen. Thomas

J. Pilgrim, who came in 1828 to teach school at Austin's colony, wrote, fifty years later, that "at that time there were more college-bred men in proportion to the population than there are now." Another observer, visiting the town of Houston in 1837, expressed surprise to find "graduates of half the major educational institutions of the United States" in that bustling village.

Stephen F. Austin, the father of Anglo-American Texas, was a quiet, bookish gentleman, who spoke, read and wrote both English and Spanish with great grace and facility. Like most educated men of his time, he also had "a little Latin and less Greek" with a smattering of French. The product of a leading Connecticut boarding school and of Transylvania University, he said he missed more than anything else, during his Texas days, the opportunity of attending the opera and theatre, and for an unlimited supply of good books. A courtly bachelor, he loved to dance, and was always popular with the ladies at the frontier balls.

Sam Houston, though limited in formal education, had served as a schoolmaster in his youth. He was a voracious reader, and wrote much poetry. Some of it was excellent. He even once had his portrait painted, posing in a classic toga, as "Caius Marius in the Ruins of Carthage."

Judge R. M. Williamson, though he is usually best remembered as a waggish, hard-drinking, fast-riding eccentric, was one of the most brilliant and polished young men of fine family to grace the early Texas scene. A victim of infantile paralysis (known then as "milk-leg"), he had grown up with a withered leg, which stuck back at a right angle from the knee. Undaunted by this handicap, he strapped a pegleg on below the knee, and had his trousers made with that leg forked, so that one part covered the withered limb and the other extended over the peg. This peculiarity won for him, from Mexican friends in his early days at San Felipe, the affectionate title of "Sënor Three-Legged Willie." The name stuck.

As a lawyer and editor, young Williamson was a firebrand in the troubles with Mexico, and was widely known as the "Patrick Henry of Texas." He commanded a ranger force during the Revolution, protecting fleeing civilians from the onrushing Mexican armies. He dashed in from this assignment on the morning of April 21, 1836, just in time to take part in the battle of San Jacinto. With his usual flair for the spectacular, Willie rode into battle that day in a suit of ragged buckskins, with a three-weeks growth of beard, and wearing a coonskin cap, fringed with nine coontails dangling from its rim. Yet he lived out his days sedately, serving as a statesman, a respected judge, and a scholarly sage consulted by the other leaders of Texas. His portrait, which hangs in our capitol, shows a handsome, polished gentleman, dressed elegantly in the style of the times.

Another spectacular figure at San Jacinto, was a handsome, black-headed young Georgian with the flamboyant name of Mirabeau Buonaparte Lamar. By the time he appeared on the San Jacinto battlefield, the 38-year-old Georgian was an accomplished orator, fencer, poet, artist, and violinist. He had been a successful newspaperman and politician, secretary to the governor and a member of the Georgia Senate. Now he was about to prove himself as a soldier.

Promoted from private to colonel on the morning of the battle, he made a dashing record. Within ten days he was secretary of war, and a month after that held a commission as a major general. (Not even the airforce has been able to match this record for rapid promotion.) His service as first elected vice-president of the Republic of Texas and the second president, insured his place in our history. He is remembered, however, as "the father of education in Texas," and for his oft-quoted statement that "the cultivated mind is the guardian genius of Democracy."

On the morning before the Battle of San Jacinto nine new recruits rowed a little boat across from Galveston Island, just in time to join the raggle-taggle Texas army. One of them later wrote of that army, as he saw it: "They were English, Irish, Scots, Mexicans, French, Germans, Italians, Poles, and Yankees, all unwashed and unshaved, their long hair and beards and mustaches matted, their clothes in tatters and plastered with mud. A more savage-looking band could scarcely have been assembled. Yet, many were gentlemen, owners of large estates. Some were distinguished for oratory, some in science, some in medicine. Many had graced famous drawing rooms."

There was no scarcity of education or sophistication in this amazing assembly. Major John Allen, of the infantry, a soldier of fortune, had fought in the Greek Revolution, and had been with the great Lord Byron when he died. Of the five men who actually fired the two small Texas cannons, "The Twin Sisters," Tom Green and Ben McCulloch, were later to be generals of the Confederacy. Green, incidentally, was a graduate of both the University of Virginia and Princeton College. Another, Scurry Richardson, was a lawyer who would later serve in both the Texas and U. S. Congresses. The fourth, Temple Overton Harris, was the scion of a distinguished Virginia family and husband of a great-niece of Mrs. Andrew Jackson. The fifth gunner, John M. Wade, was a printer who had learned his trade in New York, sticking type by hand alongside two other apprentices named Horace Greeley and George W. Kendall.

The Poles were represented by several former top-rank officers who were refugees from the ill-fated Polish Revolution of 1830. When that revolution failed, they had fled a Russian pogrom, first to Austria, then to New York. When they heard of war brewing in Texas, these professional soldiers came on the run, and rendered fine service.

There were many German settlers, including Robert Justus Kleberg, a graduate of the University of Goettingen, from which he held a doctorate of Law.

George Erath, product of leading Viennese schools, surveyor, Indian fighter, scientist, and linguist, was a private that day. The Scots, Irish, English, and French were all represented, as were the Italians. There was a company of Mexican Texans under the command of wealthy, well-educated, young Juan Seguin. And, there were at least two Negro Texans in the fighting. One was Hendricks Arnold, who had been cited for bravery at the Siege of Bexar. He served in the spy company with his hunting companions, Henry Wax Karnes and Deaf Smith. The other was a freedman named Dick, from New Orleans, who beat the drum in the four-piece Texas band. Of the three fifers who made up the rest of the band, one was a Czech and the other two were Irish. The unlikely tune they struck up to pace the Texans' charge into one of the briefest and bloodiest battles of history, was a lilting Irish love song, slightly bawdy in nature. It was "Will You Come to the Bower," by Sir Thomas Moore.

The cosmopolitan makeup of the little Texas Army at San Jacinto is simply a pat example of what Texas was like then, and has been ever since. People of all kinds, from all parts of the world have come here over the years to become Texans and to play their roles in our development. They have included titled aristocrats like Prince Solms-Braunfels and Baron Johann Ottfried von Meusebach from Germany, or Baron Tweedmouth and the Earl of Aylesworth from England, or Count Telfner and the Marquis de Sant Angelo from Italy—and bogus aristocrats like the absconding Dutch tax collector, Hendrick Nering Bögel, who called himself the Baron de Bastrop.

The first Texan to become a genuine wheeler-dealer in high finance was a Swede, the first of his countrymen to settle here. He started as a clerk in a store at Columbia in 1838, and by the time of the Civil War was one of the most powerful financiers in Texas. He worked closely with his friend, Sam Houston, in an effort to keep Texas from seceding from the Union, and when this failed, had to flee to Mexico. From there he went to New Orleans, made another fortune in plantations and sugar, then moved to New York. By the turn of the century this Swedish Texan was a genuine tycoon, building railroads and owning one of the most powerful banks on the Eastern seaboard. The Swenson bank is still an important one in New York financial circles. The immigrant boy, Swen Magnus Swenson, is best remem-

bered in Texas for his SMS ranches still operated by the family, in three West Texas counties. His bibliophile uncle, Svante Palm, gave the University of Texas its first great rare book collection.

The mark of these many nationalities is strong on the Texas landscape. The German settlements of Fredericksburg and New Braufels, or of Round Top, New Ulm and Oldenberg, still have much of the old-country flavor in their architecture, their foods, and even in the customs and speech of their older citizens. In the town of Dannevang, in South Texas, pure Danish is spoken today. Castroville, near San Antonio, is typically Alsatian. In Central Texas, above Waco, there is a cluster of small towns—Meridian, Granfills Gap and Norse—which preserve the flavor of the Norwegian ancestry of the inhabitants. The town of Round Rock, near Austin, has many fine old Swedish houses, and the names on the mailboxes throughout that area are mostly of Swedish origin. Panna Maria, in Karnes County, southeast of San Antonio, is the oldest Polish settlement in North America. Of the two Wendish colonies in the world today, one is in Australia and the other is near Giddings, in Central Texas. For years the Wendish language was preserved in this community and a newspaper was published, partly in this rare old Serbian tongue.

In the Brazos Valley, in the stretch of rich bottomlands from Hearne to Navasota, is the largest Italian farming colony in this part of the world. Around Bremond, just a little farther north, the predominant immigrant stock was Polish. Throughout this area, the Czech influence is strong, as it is throughout all the blacklands of Texas. Less well known is the fact that the first large migration of Chinese to Texas brought some 400 Chinamen to Calvert in 1870, to build the railroad from that point to Dallas. When the line was completed in 1874, many of them came back to that fertile region and settled. Few are left, today. They have drifted to the cities. The ancient royal Spanish highway, the Camino Real, cuts across Texas from San Antonio to Nacogdoches. At the point just east of the Brazos where it intersects a more modern highway from Houston to Dallas, there is a crossroads store and a few houses. This place is known today as Benchley, named in honor of the railroad conductor grandfather of humorist Robert Benchley. Originally called Stagger Point, it is one of the oldest Irish settlements in Texas.

The Japanese were invited into the Gulf Coast area around the turn of the century, to teach Texans how to raise rice profitably. From the example of such enterprising and well-educated gentlemen as the heads of the Saibara and Kishi families, Texans learned well. Rice is now one of the principal crops of the Gulf Coast area.

One of the most spectacular contributions to the Texas scene is being made by the Lebanese, comparative newcomers. Fleeing the oppression of the Ottoman empire, they came here with only their bare hands and their willingness to work. Most Lebanese started in Texas as peddlers, carrying packs from door to door. As they acquired a little capital, they opened stores. Then they made the money to educate their children. From the first generation of children of these immigrants, have come some spectacular Texans, like Mike Halbouty, one of the most erudite and effective leaders in the oil industry today, and Mike DeBakey, whose magic with heart surgery is known the world around. Then there are the Haggar and Farah families of El Paso, both of whom have developed clothing manufacturing businesses of world-wide proportions; the Kadanes who pioneered oil development in Northwest Texas; and the Ferris family who produced the scholarly translator and interpreter of the works of Kahlil Gibran.

Texas has truly been the meeting ground of many cultures, and has been enriched by them all. In turn, it has supplied a comparatively free society, with a growing economy, based on vast resources, in which these diverse peoples could all find their own places and produce their own successes in their own way.

This discussion has ignored from 10,000 to 40,000 years of human history in Texas, being confined to the period which began about 1820 with the intrusion of the Anglo-Americans. These immigrants from the United States of the North have so dominated our politics and our economy that many historians are prone to think of their history as Texas history.

This is not true, of course. Somewhere around the end of the last Ice Age, men began to drift into Texas and to settle. They, like all who came after them, were immigrants, generally believed to have been of Asiatic origin. In the 300 years immediately preceding the Anglo-American intrusion of the 1800's, others came — Spaniards, Negroes, Italians, a few Irishmen and Scots — and many Mexicans. These people laid the groundwork for later Texas. They brought the first cattle, the first horses, many of the first crops and trees. They had established civilized centers here, with a well-developed ranching economy, long before the Austins spearheaded the flood of immigration from east of the Sabine.

My reason for ignoring this important basis of our history and culture springs from the fact that the Texian myth, as we know it, like many of our other institutions, came with the Anglo flood. Before 1821 there was no Texas myth. The very term "Texian" did not arrive until 1835, and then it was the creation of an editorial writer for the *New Orleans Bee*, whose idea was reprinted and endorsed by Gail Borden, editor of Texas' leading newspaper.

It is amazing that Texas, which had been Spanish in name for three centuries and Mexican in fact for nearly two, should, within a few years become predominantly Anglo, and remain that way for the rest of its history. It is ridiculous to fall back on the old myth of Anglo superiority for an explanation. This is a fallacy which has made us very unpopular with our neighbors, while also deluding our own children.

There are a few simple and logical explanations for the inundation of Texas by people from the United States, and for the domination of the Texas political and economic scene from that time on by this particular group. These explanations are based, not on ethnological myth, but on historical circumstances.

Since a few years after their revolt from England, the former British colonists had been pushing westward at a breathtaking pace, hurdling mountain chains, rivers, and forests, to gobble up new land. By 1821, when Texas was opened to them, they had three generations of frontiering experience behind them, and were the only people in the world so equipped. Suddenly, in 1820, on the heels of a paralyzing money panic, the United States had adopted a new law concerning the public lands. In the past the frontiersman had been able to move into a new country, tame it and clear out the Indians, then lay claim to the land for a token down payment and a vague promise of future payments. By the time his land was developed and people started moving in around him, to increase the market and values, he could sell out at a good profit and move on. If for some reason his enterprise had failed, he simply abandoned the land, forgot the small investment, and rode over the hill. The Anglo-American frontiersman had thus learned to exploit the land, to look upon it as something to buy and sell, trade and abandon. This was an entirely new concept. Both the Mexicans and the old-world immigrants had been trained to look on land as a permanent thing — the one solid base for the establishment of a family and fortune. They acquired a piece of land, stayed with it, raised their families then divided the land among their offspring. If the land was fruitful and the seasons favorable, they became wealthy. If the land was poor, they simply remained poor, but they stayed regardless of circumstance.

The new U. S. land law of 1820 required that anyone who took up the public lands could do so at a price of $1.25 an acre, cash. There was no credit. With the country strapped by a panic, this brought the entire frontiering movement to a grinding halt. The opening of Texas lands, at this moment, offering approximately 5,000 acres per family, for only the cost of surveying, seemed like the answer to prayer for the frustrated frontiersman. Here was good, rich land in a hospitable climate, free for the taking. And he swarmed across the border.

Another major factor in the preponderance of Anglo-American immigration over that from Mexico and Europe during this period was geographic.

The immigrants who came to newly-opened Texas from Mexico and Europe were far more sought-after and more warmly welcomed by the Spanish and Mexican governments, but their numbers remained small in comparison with the flood of land-seekers from the United States. To reach Texas, the European had to make a long, hazardous and expensive sea journey. The Mexican, in coming from the settled areas of his country, had to cross wild mountain ranges and several hundred miles of barren desert. Even after he forded the Rio Bravo, he faced a trek across an inhospitable semi-desert for a hundred miles or more, before he reached fertile, well-watered lands suitable for homesteading.

The Anglo, on the other hand, could simply ford the Red or the Sabine, coming out of a green well-forested, well-watered section into the Piney Woods of East Texas—green, well-forested and well-watered. He was as much at home on one side of the river as on the other.

The Germans, the Poles, the Italians, the French and the Mexicans came to Texas in this period, but they were far outnumbered by the Anglos. When they got here, the people from other lands simply took up a piece of land and held onto it. The Anglos, trained by their national experience, swarmed in, took up land, bought and sold it, and moved on through to establish ever-new frontiers.

When the Revolution came in 1836, the Anglo-Americans outnumbered other immigrants appreciably, but not nearly enough to dominate the Convention of 1836 and the government of the ensuing Republic as they did.

Again, historic circumstance gave them the upper hand. Of all the people who were in Texas at that time, only the Anglo-Americans had back of them three generations of successful experience in revolution and the establishment of self-government. The colonists included a handful of actual veterans of Washington's Army. (The graves of a dozen or so have been positively identified in Texas.) Many, like Sam Houston, were the sons of men who fought the British in the 1770's. Others, like R. M. (Three-Legged Willie) Williamson and Mirabeau Buonaparte Lamar, were grandsons.

Many, in their frontiering adventures, had taken part in the establishment of territorial and state governments. They had served in constitutional conventions, in legislatures, as attorney general and several had been members of the United States Congress. They had the know-how.

When the Convention of 1836 was called, the Anglo-Americans, because of this experience, were elected delegates. When the Convention met, they took it over, decided its issues and wrote both the Declaration of Independence and the first Constitution. From that point on, Texas became predominantly an Anglo-American area, so far as political, economic and associated factors are concerned. Culturally, however, the state has remained diverse, with a heritage enriched by the cultures of many lands.

Texas may well be one of the most culturally-advantaged spots in the world today. Historic circumstance has brought together, in a vast, rich and amazingly diverse area, people of many nationalities, races and cultures. They have had an opportunity to live together, work together and grow together, without overcrowding, or over-competitive scrambling for the means of existence. An expanding economy has provided a free society, in which individuals from every group have found an opportunity to grow and prosper, and to contribute to the total development of Texas.

Texans always have been, as they are today, all kinds of people. There are Anglo Texans, Chinese Texans, Greek Texans, and more than a score of other kinds. All are Texans. They and their people have contributed to making Texas whatever it is today, good or bad.

Whatever Texas becomes tomorrow will be the result of their successes and failures—not as members of any particular ethnic group, but as individuals.

Flight of Apollo 11, July 20, 1969

hour 109:20

ARMSTRONG   Houston, this is Neil. Radio check.

CAPCOM   Neil, this Houston. You're loud and clear. Break, break. Buzz, this is Houston. Radio check and verify TV circuit breaker in.

ALDRIN   Roger, TV circuit breaker's in. Receive loud and clear.

CAPCOM   Man, we're getting a picture on the TV.

ALDRIN   Oh, you've got a good picture, huh?

CAPCOM   There's a great deal of contrast in it, and currently it's upside-down on our monitor. But we can make out a fair amount of detail.

ALDRIN   Okay, will you verify the opening I ought to have on the camera.

CAPCOM   Stand by.

CAPCOM   Okay, Neil, we can see you coming down the ladder now.

ARMSTRONG   Okay, I just checked that first step, Buzz. It's not collapsed too far, but it's adequate to get back up.

CAPCOM   Roger, we copy.

ARMSTRONG   It'll take a pretty good little jump.

CAPCOM   Buzz, this is Houston. F 2 1/160th second for shadow photography on the sequence camera.

ALDRIN   Okay.

ARMSTRONG   I'm at the foot of the ladder. The LM foot pads are only depressed in the surface about 1 or 2 inches. Although the surface appears to be very, very fine grained, as you get close to it. It's almost like a powder. Now and then, it's very fine.

ARMSTRONG   I'm going to step off the LM now.

ARMSTRONG   That's one small step for man. One giant leap for mankind.

ARMSTRONG   The surface is fine and powdery. I can pick it up loosely with my toe. It does adhere in fine layers like powdered charcoal to the sole and sides of my boots. I only go in a small fraction of an inch. Maybe an eighth of an inch, but I can see the footprints of my boots and treads in the fine sandy particles.

CAPCOM   Neil, this is Houston. We're copying.

END OF TAPE

These are some of the things of Texas.